CW01430677

Mango Mia

Celebrating the Tropical World of Mangoes

By

Vikas Khanna

and

Hari Nayak

ISBN 0-7414-2483-5

Published by:

INFI(∞)ITY
PUBLISHING.COM

1094 New DeHaven Street, Suite 100
West Conshohocken, PA 19428-2713
Info@buybooksontheweb.com
www.buybooksontheweb.com
Toll-free (877) BUY BOOK
Local Phone (610) 941-9999
Fax (610) 941-9959

Printed in the United States of America

Printed on Recycled Paper

Published July 2005

DEDICATION

I dedicate this book to Bindu Khanna, my mother.

-Vikas Khanna

I dedicate this book to Priyu Nayak, my wife.

-Hari Nayak

MANGO MIA

INTRODUCTION

HISTORY

Mangoes are native to southeastern Asia, where they have been grown for more than 4,000 years. Because the mango seed can't be dispersed naturally by wind or water due to its large size and weight, it is believed that people who moved from one region to another transported the fruit to new areas. The spread of Buddhism assisted in the distribution of mangoes in Southeastern Asia. Mango cultivation has now spread to many parts of the tropical and sub-tropical world, where they grow best.

Mangoes were carried to Africa during the 16th century and later found their way aboard Portuguese ships to Brazil in the 1700s. Later, in 1742, mangoes were found growing in the West Indies.

In 1860, mangoes were successfully introduced to Florida along the east coast, where only a few varieties were grown. In 1889, the United States Department of Agriculture introduced a grafted variety from India called the "Mulgoa," also known as "Mulgoba" in the United States.

WHERE ARE MANGOES GROWN?

Asia still accounts for more than three quarters of the world's mangoes, with India remaining the main producer. Did you know that India grows more mangoes than all its other fruits combined? Indonesia, Philippines and Thailand are the other main countries in the world where mangoes are grown.

Most of the mangoes sold in the United States are grown in Florida or imported from Mexico, Haiti, the Caribbean, and South America.

TOP U.S. STATE PRODUCER:
#1 = Florida

TOP WORLD PRODUCERS:
#1 = India
#2 = South America

HARVESTING

Mango trees are very tall in height and have thick, leathery leaves. From their branches, long stems hold clusters of fruits that can range from a few ounces to a few pounds.

Mangoes are harvested with the aid of a picking device attached to the end of a long bamboo pole. The picking device consists of a pair of string-operated shears and a collection sack. When picking mangoes, it is very important to leave a long stem. Immediately after being picked, all mangoes that are to be exported undergo a post harvest, hot water treatment.

Florida mangoes are harvested several times during the season. On any individual tree, fruits may be harvested daily, since the earliest bloom matures and ripens weeks before the later bloom.

Mangoes are harvested at a mature-green stage to withstand the post harvest handling steps required to bring them to market. The post harvest life of a mango usually ranges from 4-6 days.

AVAILABILITY

Mangoes grown in the U.S. (in Florida and California) are in peak season from May to September; however, imported mangoes are sporadically available throughout the year.

HOW TO SELECT AND STORE

Look for mangoes with unblemished yellow skin with a red tinge or blush. Avoid mangoes with bruises or soft spots. You can buy green mangoes and ripen them at home by placing them in a brown paper bag on your counter for 2 to 3 days. Ripe mangoes will last 2 to 3 days at room temperature or for up to 5 days in a plastic bag in the refrigerator.

NUTRITION INFORMATION

Mangoes are rich in vitamins A and C. One serving (1/2 medium mango) contains 70 calories—40% of your daily vitamin A and 15% of your daily vitamin C.

STARTERS

Thai Steak and Mango Salad

Chicken and Mango Wraps

Chilled Mango and Cucumber Soup

Mango Salad with Lemon Dressing

Tuna and Mango Sashimi Salad

Mango Pasta Salad

THAI STEAK AND MANGO SALAD

The exciting flavor of Thai basil with crisp crunchy green mango and tender sirloin steak creates this refreshing textured salad.

SERVES 4

3 cloves garlic, minced
5 sprigs cilantro (reserve leaves)
5 sprigs Thai basil
1 teaspoon freshly ground black pepper
3 tablespoons peanut oil
12 ounces sirloin steak
1 small Bibb lettuce, washed and dried
1 cucumber, peeled, seeded and diced
1 small firm ripe mango, peeled, cut from the pit and diced
4 large green onions, chopped
2 tablespoons Thai fish sauce
2 tablespoons freshly squeezed lime juice
1 tablespoon soy sauce
2 teaspoons minced Thai red chili
2 teaspoons packed brown sugar

METHOD

In a food processor, grind the garlic, cilantro stems, Thai basil, salt, pepper and 2 tbsp of the oil into a smooth paste. Marinate the steak with paste on both sides.

In a large heavy skillet, cook the steak 3 to 4 minutes on each side for medium rare. Let it cool.

Cut the steak into thin strips. This could be served family style by tossing the lettuce leaves, mango, cucumber and green onions. Arrange the steak strips on top.

In a small bowl, combine fish sauce, lime juice, soy sauce, red chili and brown sugar and stir until the sugar is dissolved.

To serve, drizzle the salad with dressing and garnish with cilantro leaves.

CHICKEN AND MANGO WRAPS

This dish combines the sweetness of the mango with the delicate flavor of Thai basil.

Shrimp is an excellent substitute for the chicken.

SERVES 4

1/3 cup sour cream
1/3 cup mayonnaise
1/4 cup chopped fresh Thai basil
2 tablespoons chopped fresh chives
2 1/4 teaspoons salt
1/4 teaspoon black pepper
1 tablespoon fresh lemon juice
2 grilled cold chicken breasts
1 (1-lb) firm-ripe mango, peeled and cut into 1/3-inch cubes
4 (10-inch) flour tortillas
1 (6-oz) bunch watercress, tough stems discarded

METHOD

Pulse sour cream, mayonnaise, Thai basil, chives, 1/4 teaspoon salt, and pepper in a blender until herbs are finely chopped and mixture is pale green.

Dice the grilled chicken breasts into small cubes. Mix the green paste with the chicken to create a chicken salad.

Toast tortillas 1 at a time directly on burner (gas or electric) at moderately high heat, turning over and rotating with tongs, until puffed slightly and browned in spots but still flexible, 30 to 40 seconds. Transfer to a clean kitchen towel as toasted and stack, loosely wrapped, in towel.

Divide watercress among tortillas, arranging it across middle, then top with 1 1/4 cups chicken salad. Tuck in ends of wraps, then roll up tightly to enclose filling. Cut wraps in half diagonally.

Serve with the Thai mayonnaise as a dipping sauce.

CHILLED MANGO AND CUCUMBER SOUP

SERVES 7

2 medium-size ripe mangoes, peeled and pitted
2 English cucumbers (1 1/2 pounds total)
1/4 cup water, plus 2 cups
3 tablespoons finely chopped red onion
3 tablespoons fresh lime juice, or to taste
2 tablespoons chopped fresh cilantro leaves
1 1/2 teaspoons salt

METHOD

Finely chop 1 mango and 1 cucumber and set aside. Coarsely chop remaining mango and cucumber and purée with 1/4 cup water in a blender until almost smooth. Transfer to a bowl and stir in finely chopped mango and cucumber, onion, lime juice, and 2 cups cold water. Place bowl in a larger bowl of ice and cold water and stir until cool.

Just before serving, stir in cilantro and 1 1/4 teaspoons salt.

MANGO SALAD WITH LEMON DRESSING

A refreshing salad and can be served as a side for grilled meats.

SERVES 4

2 teaspoons balsamic vinegar
2 teaspoons fresh lemon juice
1 teaspoon sugar
1/2 teaspoon salt
1/4 teaspoon black pepper
3 tablespoons extra-virgin olive oil
1 (1-lb) firm-ripe mango, peeled and cut into 1/2-inch cubes
1 large tomato, cut into 1/2-inch cubes
1 small red onion, halved lengthwise and thinly sliced crosswise
1/3 cup fresh cilantro leaves

METHOD

Whisk together vinegar, lemon juice, sugar, salt, and pepper until sugar is dissolved, then add oil, whisking until emulsified. Add remaining ingredients and toss until coated.

TUNA AND MANGO SASHIMI SALAD

This is a very refreshing salad with the Hawaiian flavors.

SERVES 4

16 ounces sashimi quality tuna steak
2 tablespoons finely chopped green onion
2 tablespoons chopped cilantro
3 tablespoons soy sauce
1 tablespoon minced Thai chili
1 teaspoon minced garlic
2 tablespoons minced fresh ginger
2 tablespoons sesame oil
1 large ripe mango, cut into 1-inch cubes
1 tablespoon sesame seeds

METHOD

Cut the tuna into 1-inch cubes and place in a medium bowl. Add green onion, cilantro, soy sauce, and chili. In a small bowl, combine the garlic and ginger.

In a small saucepan, heat the sesame oil until it starts to smoke. Pour into the ginger garlic mixture and mix well. Pour the ginger garlic mixture to the tuna and mix well and evenly coat it. Cover and refrigerate for 2 hours.

To serve, carefully fold the mango into the tuna mixture. Garnish with toasted sesame seeds.

MANGO PASTA SALAD

SERVES 6

1 cup canned chickpeas, drained

1/2 cup liverwurst, diced

1/2 cup mangoes, peeled and cut into thin wedges

3 cups mixed frozen vegetables, defrosted (peas, carrots, corn)

1 cup smooth peanut butter, melted

3 cups yogurt

1 cup cooked fusilli or any pasta, cooled

salt and pepper, to taste

lettuce leaves, to serve

METHOD

Combine chickpeas, liverwurst, mangoes, peas, carrots, corn, smooth peanut butter, yogurt, fusilli, and seasoning. Arrange lettuce leaves on a platter. Spoon the pea mango mixture on top. Serve chilled.

MAIN COURSES

Mango and Shrimp Skewers

Canton Beef with Stir-Fried Vegetables and Mango

Pork Chops with Mango Relish

Grilled Tuna Steaks with Mango Habanero Mojo

Mango Marinated Roast Chicken

Grilled Medallions of Beef with Mango White Balsamic Vinegar Reduction

Masala Mango Sloppy Joes

Fish Curry with Green Mango

Pan-Seared Snapper with Honey Mango Sauce

Spiced Lamb Chops with Mango Mint Sauce

Grilled Lobster with Sweet and Sour Mango Curry

Salmon with Mango Chile Salsa

Curried Chicken with Mango Sandwiches

Pork Tenderloin with Mango Chutney

Scallops with Bell Peppers, Avocado, and Mangoes

Grilled Oysters with Mango Pico de Gallo

BBQ Burger with Mango Ketchup

MANGO AND SHRIMP SKEWERS

SERVES 6

3 tablespoons olive oil

1 tablespoon minced peeled fresh ginger

2 garlic cloves, minced

1 teaspoon dried crushed red pepper

18 uncooked colossal shrimp or 36 jumbo shrimp (about 2 pounds), peeled, tails left intact, de-veined

2 red bell peppers, each cut into 12 pieces

2 firm but ripe mangoes, peeled, pitted, each cut into 12 wedges

6 12-inch bamboo skewers (for colossal shrimp) or twelve 12-inch bamboo skewers (for jumbo shrimp), soaked in water 30 minutes, drained

METHOD

Mix first 4 ingredients in large bowl. Add shrimp, bell peppers, and mangoes; toss to coat. Alternate bell pepper, mango, and 3 colossal shrimp on each of 6 skewers, or alternate bell pepper, mango, and 3 jumbo shrimp on each of 12 skewers. (Can be prepared 4 hours ahead.) Cover and chill.

Grill shrimp on medium heat until cooked through, cooking colossal shrimp about 4 minutes per side and jumbo shrimp about 3 minutes per side. Serve hot.

CANTON BEEF WITH STIR-FRIED VEGETABLES AND MANGO

SERVES 4

For Marinade

2 tablespoons soy sauce
2 tablespoons water
1 teaspoon cornstarch
1 teaspoon hot chili oil
1 teaspoon minced garlic

For Beef

1 pound top sirloin steak, about 1-inch thick, cut into 1/2-inch strips about 2 or 3 inches long

For Stir Fry

4 Chinese dried mushrooms or 8 fresh shitakes, stemmed and sliced
4 tablespoons peanut oil
1 red pepper, seeded and julienne
1 carrot, cut in half lengthwise and sliced on a diagonal
1/4 cup bamboo shoots, drained and julienne
2 scallions, sliced on a diagonal
2 tablespoons water
1 mango, peeled, pitted, and julienne

METHOD

Combine all the ingredients for the marinade in a mixing bowl. Add the sliced steak and let sit at room temperature for 1 hour or refrigerate overnight.

Soak the mushrooms in warm water for 15 minutes. Drain and squeeze gently to remove the excess moisture. Remove the stalks and dice. Heat 2 tablespoons of the oil in a wok or deep skillet. Remove the beef from the marinade and pat dry. Quickly stir-fry the beef in 2 or 3 batches over high heat for about 2 minutes, until well browned on all sides, but rare or medium-rare inside. Remove the beef and keep warm.

Wipe out the wok with a paper towel and heat the remaining 2 tablespoons of oil. Add the diced mushrooms, bell peppers, carrots, bamboo shoots, and scallions and stir-fry for a few seconds over high heat. Carefully add the water to steam the vegetables and stir until it has evaporated. Add the mango and reserved beef, warm through, and remove from the heat.

Spoon a bed of the rice onto warm serving plates and top with the stir-fry. Serve immediately.

PORK CHOPS WITH MANGO RELISH

SERVES 4

For the Pork Chops

2 tablespoons fat-free plain yogurt
2 teaspoons honey
2 garlic cloves, minced
1 teaspoon white wine vinegar or cider vinegar
1/2 teaspoon ground cumin
1/4 teaspoon salt
1/2 teaspoon ground turmeric
1/4 teaspoon ground cloves
1/4 teaspoon ground cinnamon
1/4 teaspoon cayenne pepper
1/2 teaspoon minced fresh gingerroot
4 boneless pork loin chops (4 ounces each)

For Mango Relish

1 ripe mango, peeled, pitted, and cut into very small dice
3/4 cup chopped red onion
3/4 cup chopped seeded tomatoes
4 teaspoons chopped seeded jalapeno pepper
2 teaspoons lime juice
salt to taste

METHOD

In a large resealable plastic bag, combine the first 11 ingredients. Add pork. Seal bag and turn to coat; refrigerate for at least 2 hours.

Meanwhile, combine the relish ingredients in a bowl. Let stand at room temperature for 1 hour; refrigerate until serving.

Grill pork chops, covered, over medium heat or broil 3-4 inches from the heat for 6-10 minutes on each side or until a meat thermometer reads 160 degrees F. Serve with mango relish.

GRILLED TUNA STEAKS WITH MANGO HABANERO MOJO

The floral note of the habaneros is a tremendous partner to the mango, but if you can't find them, substitute another spicy chili. This mojo is also delicious with grilled shrimp or pork.

SERVES 4

For the Tuna and Marinade

1/4 cup finely chopped fresh flat parsley
1/2 cup finely chopped fresh cilantro
2 cloves garlic, minced
1/4 cup dry sherry
1/4 cup olive oil
1 teaspoon kosher salt, more for the seasoning
freshly ground black pepper to taste
4 tuna steaks, 6 ounces each

For the Mojo

1 ripe, juicy mango, peeled and pitted
1/4 cup Chardonnay or other dry white wine
juice of 1/2 orange (about 1/4 cup)
1/2 teaspoon minced habanero, Scotch bonnet, or other hot chili (seeds removed)
sprigs of cilantro for garnish

METHOD

In a large shallow dish, mix the parsley, cilantro, garlic, sherry, olive oil, salt, and pepper. Add the tuna and toss to thoroughly coat, pressing the herbs all over the steaks. Let it sit for 30 minutes.

In a blender, combine the mango, Chardonnay, and orange juice. Stir in the habanero and set aside. (This mojo is served at room temperature or very slightly warmed - don't boil it.)

Light a charcoal or gas grill. When the grill is very hot, remove the tuna from the marinade and slightly season it with salt and pepper. Sear the tuna for 3 to 5 minutes on each side for medium rare (or more, depending on the thickness of the tuna).

Drizzle some mojo on each plate, set the tuna on the mojo, drizzle on a little more mojo, and garnish with cilantro.

MANGO MARINATED ROAST CHICKEN

SERVES 4

1/2 small onion, coarse
1/2 cup chopped green onions
1 medium habanero chile or jalapeno chile, seeded if desired
2 tablespoons canola oil
1 tablespoon cider vinegar
1 tablespoon chopped fresh thyme
1 tablespoon kosher salt
1 tablespoon ground black pepper
1 tablespoon sugar
1 tablespoon ground allspice
1/2 teaspoon grated nutmeg
1/2 teaspoon ground cinnamon
1/2 cup puréed mango
one 4-pound whole chicken, wing tips tucked under

METHOD

Puree first 13 ingredients in the food processor until smooth. Place chicken in large glass or ceramic bowl. Rub marinade all over the chicken and inside body cavity. Marinate at least for an hour.

Preheat oven to 375 degrees F.

Place chicken, breast side up, on rack set in large roasting pan. Add 1 cup water to pan to prevent pan drippings from scorching. Roast chicken 30 minutes. Turn chicken over (back side up) and roast 30 minutes. Turn chicken over again (breast side up), and roast until chicken is golden brown and the instant-read meat thermometer registers 160 degrees F when inserted into innermost part of thigh, about 30 minutes longer.

Transfer chicken to platter. Serve it hot with Mango Salad.

GRILLED MEDALLIONS OF BEEF WITH MANGO WHITE BALSAMIC VINEGAR REDUCTION

<u>SERVES 4</u>

For the Marinade

3 tablespoons vegetable oil
2 tablespoons minced onion
2 tablespoons minced fresh ginger
1 tablespoon curry powder
1/4 cup lime juice
1/4 cup chopped mangoes
/4 cup honey
4 medallions beef tenderloin, 1 1/2 inches thick

For the Sauce

2 tablespoons vegetable oil
1/4 cup chopped shallots
1/4 cup white wine
1 tablespoon sugar dissolved in 2 tablespoons warm water
1/2 cup puréed mango
1/4 cup beef stock
1/4 cup white balsamic vinegar

<u>METHOD</u>

Place the first 7 ingredients into a shallow bowl or baking pan, mix together, then add the beef medallions, and allow them to marinate at room temperature for 30 minutes.

In a sauté pan over medium heat, warm the vegetable oil. Add the shallots and cook, stirring, for a minute. Add the white wine, sugar and water mixture, puréed mango, beef stock, and vinegar. Reduce and simmer uncovered for 25-30 minutes until the sauce thickens.

Remove the beef medallions from the marinade and grill until they are cooked to the point of doneness that you prefer.

Place the medallions on serving plates and pour the warm sauce on top.

MASALA MANGO SLOPPY JOES

Sloppy Joes—hamburger bun sandwiches filled with ground beef and onions in a tomato sauce—are, as the name implies, a little untidy to eat. In this recipe, we use pita pockets, which make for neater and more convenient sandwiches. We further tweaked this American classic by using masala, the name for a wide variety of spice blends used in Indian cuisine. Here, we combine mango, chili powder, black pepper, ground coriander, and turmeric in an aromatic masala, resulting in an altogether "grown-up" version of a favorite from childhood.

SERVES 4

3 tablespoons butter
2 onions, chopped
3 garlic cloves, minced
3 teaspoons minced ginger
1 pound lean high-quality ground beef
2 Roma tomatoes, chopped
3/4 cup corn kernels (from 1 ear of corn)
4 teaspoons freshly ground black pepper
1 tablespoon pure red chili powder
1 tablespoon ground coriander
1/2 teaspoon turmeric
salt to taste
1/2 cup beef stock or water
4 pita breads
1/2 lime
1 mango, peeled, pitted, and chopped

METHOD

Preheat the oven to 300 degrees F.

Melt the butter in a large skillet. Add the onions and sauté over medium heat for 7 to 10 minutes, or until golden brown. Add the garlic and ginger and sauté for 2 to 3 minutes longer. Add the beef and cook for about 5 minutes or until just browned, using a kitchen fork to break up any lumps. Carefully pour off any fat in the pan.

Add the tomatoes, corn, pepper, chile powder, coriander, turmeric, and salt, and sauté for 3 to 4 minutes, stirring occasionally. Reduce the heat to low, add the beef stock and simmer for about 10 minutes, or until the mixture is moist but not soupy. In the meantime, wrap the pitas in aluminum foil and warm them in the oven. Remove the beef from the heat and season with salt and pepper. Fold in chopped mangoes.

FISH CURRY WITH GREEN MANGO

The green (unripe) mango adds a sour element to this fish curry.

SERVES 4

1 cup finely grated dried unsweetened coconut
1/4 cup finely chopped onion
16 curry leaves
1/2 teaspoon ground coriander
1/4 teaspoon cayenne pepper
1/8 teaspoon turmeric
1 cup water
3/4 teaspoon salt
1 1/2 pounds swordfish steaks (1-inch thick), skinned and cut into cubes
3/4 cup slivered green mangoes with skin
1 Serrano or Thai chile, thinly sliced

METHOD

In a food processor or blender, combine the coconut, onion, and 8 of the curry leaves with the coriander, cayenne, and turmeric. Add 1/2 cup of the water and process to a paste.

In a large deep skillet, combine the coconut paste and salt with the remaining 1/2 cup of water. Add the swordfish in a single layer and bring to a boil. Add the mango, chile, and the remaining 8 curry leaves. Gently turn each piece of fish and simmer over low heat until just cooked through, about 10 minutes.

Serve immediately.

PAN-SEARED SNAPPER WITH HONEY MANGO SAUCE

SERVES 6

For Fish

2 tablespoons barbecue sauce
2 tablespoons vegetable oil
six 6-ounce red snapper or Chilean sea bass fillets

For Sauce

1 tablespoon vegetable oil
1/3 cup finely chopped onion
1 cup diced fresh mango
1 cup orange juice
1 teaspoon chopped fresh habanero or scotch bonnet pepper
1 tablespoon clover honey
salt to taste
vegetable oil cooking spray for cooking the fish

METHOD

In a glass or porcelain dish, combine the barbecue sauce with the vegetable oil. Dip both sides of the fish fillets into the mixture, cover and set aside at room temperature.

In a medium non-stick skillet over moderate heat, heat the vegetable oil. Add the onion, lower the heat, cover and cook for about 5 minutes or until the onion is tender. Add the mango, orange juice, hot pepper, and honey and cook, over medium heat, uncovered for 5 minutes. Remove from the heat and cool for a few minutes. In a blender or food processor purée the mixture. Turn off the heat and return the puréed sauce to the pan, and season to taste with salt.

Lightly spray a 10-inch, non-stick skillet with vegetable spray and set the skillet over medium heat for 1 minute. Cook the snapper fillets for 2 to 3 minutes per side or until just cooked through. Serve it hot with mango honey sauce.

SPICED LAMB CHOPS WITH MANGO MINT SAUCE

SERVES 8

Mango-Mint Sauce

2 1-pound ripe mangoes, peeled, seeded
2 cups fresh mint leaves
4 green onions, cut into 1-inch pieces
2 tablespoons fresh lime juice
2 Serrano chilies, halved, seeded

Lamb Chops

1 1/2 tablespoons ground cumin
1 1/2 tablespoons ground coriander
1 tablespoon coarse kosher salt
1 1/2 teaspoons ground cinnamon
1 teaspoon turmeric
1/2 teaspoon cayenne pepper
1/2 teaspoon ground cardamom
1/8 teaspoon ground cloves
1/4 cup olive oil
2 garlic cloves, chopped
16 1-inch thick, lamb loin chops
fresh mint sprigs

METHOD

Blend all ingredients of the sauce in a food processor until smooth. Transfer to small bowl. Season it with salt. Cover and chill. (Can be made 1 day ahead.)

Prepare barbecue (medium-high heat). Whisk first 8 ingredients in small bowl. Mix oil and garlic in another bowl. Brush chops on both sides with oil mixture, and then press chops into spice mixture to coat both sides. Grill chops to desired doneness, about 4 minutes per side for medium-rare. Transfer to platter. Garnish with mint sprigs. Serve warm or at room temperature with sauce.

GRILLED LOBSTER WITH SWEET AND SOUR MANGO CURRY

SERVES 4

1 ripe mango, peeled, pitted, and cut into very small dice
3 tablespoons fresh lime juice
1 tablespoon minced fresh ginger
2 teaspoons curry powder
3 tablespoons chopped fresh chives
2 tablespoons minced shallots
white pepper
8 ounces green beans cut in half
8 ounces asparagus
1/2 red bell pepper, thinly sliced
8 cups mixed baby greens
1/2 cup fresh cilantro leaves
white pepper
1 1/4 pounds cooked lobster tail meat sliced into medallions
16 yellow baby plum tomatoes or cherry tomatoes

METHOD

Place first 4 ingredients in blender. Blend until smooth. Stir in chives and shallots. Season to taste with salt and white pepper. This dressing can be prepared 1 day ahead. Cover and refrigerate.

Bring heavy large saucepan of water to boil. Add beans and cook until tender, about 4 minutes. Using slotted spoon, transfer to bowl of cold water. Drain. Repeat process with asparagus. Cut asparagus, beans, bell pepper, greens, and cilantro in large bowl. Drizzle some dressing over and toss lightly. Season it with salt and white pepper to taste.

Arrange salad on plates. Fan lobster decoratively.

Garnish with tomatoes and drizzle remaining dressing over.

SALMON WITH MANGO CHILE SALSA

SERVES 2

1 10-ounce mango, peeled, pitted, and diced
1/4 cup chopped fresh cilantro
1/4 cup chopped red onion
1 tablespoon fresh lime juice
2 teaspoons minced seeded serrano chili
1 teaspoon grated lime peel
1 garlic clove, finely chopped
2 tablespoons olive oil
2 6-ounce salmon fillets

METHOD

Prepare barbecue (medium-high heat). Combine first 7 ingredients in small bowl; mix in 1 1/2 tablespoons oil. Season the salsa with salt and pepper. Brush salmon with remaining 1/2 tablespoon oil.

Grill until just opaque in center, about 5 minutes per side. Serve with salsa.

CURRIED CHICKEN WITH MANGO SANDWICHES

SERVES 2

1/4 cup mayonnaise
1 tablespoon sour cream
1 1/2 teaspoons chopped fresh cilantro leaves
1 teaspoon curry powder
1/2 firm-ripe mango
2 skinless boneless chicken breast halves (about 3/4 pound total)
1 teaspoon olive oil
1 7-inch length soft Italian bread, such as ciabatta
4 small soft-leafed lettuce leaves

METHOD

In a bowl, stir together mayonnaise, sour cream, cilantro, curry powder, and salt and pepper to taste until combined well. Peel mango and thinly slice lengthwise.

Pat chicken dry and season with salt and pepper. In a 9-inch nonstick skillet heat oil over moderately high heat until hot, but not smoking, and sauté chicken 4 minutes on each side, or until cooked through. Transfer chicken to a cutting board and let stand 5 minutes. Diagonally slice chicken and season with salt and pepper.

Horizontally halve bread with a serrated knife and spread cut sides with mayonnaise mixture. On 1 bread half, stack lettuce, chicken, and mango and top with remaining bread half, gently pressing together. Cut sandwich in half.

41

PORK TENDERLOIN WITH MANGO CHUTNEY

SERVES 6

1 tablespoon vegetable oil
1/2 teaspoon cumin seeds
1 cup chopped onion
1 tablespoon chopped, peeled fresh ginger
1 large firm but ripe mango, peeled, pitted, chopped
(about 1 cup)
1 tablespoon chopped, seeded jalapeno chili
1/4 teaspoon ground turmeric
2 tablespoons fresh lime juice
nonstick vegetable oil spray
2 12-ounce pork tenderloins, trimmed
1 tablespoon curry powder
2 tablespoons fresh cilantro leaves

METHOD

Heat oil in large nonstick skillet over medium heat. Add
cumin seeds; stir until brown, about 2 minutes. Add
onion and ginger to skillet; sauté until onion begins to
brown, about 5 minutes. Add mango, jalapeno, and
turmeric. Stir until mango is heated through, about 3
minutes. Cool slightly. Mix in the lime juice. Season the
chutney with salt and pepper. (Can be made 6 hours
ahead.) Cover and chill. Bring to room temperature
before serving.

Spray barbecue grill with vegetable oil spray. Prepare
barbecue (medium-high heat) or preheat broiler. Rub all
sides of pork with curry powder; sprinkle with salt and
pepper. Grill or broil pork until thermometer inserted
into thickest part of pork registers 155 degrees F.
Turning frequently, about 20 minutes if grilling or 15

minutes if broiling. Transfer pork to work surface. Cut pork crosswise into 1/2-inch thick slices. Transfer to plates. Sprinkle with cilantro.

Serve with chutney.

SCALLOPS WITH BELL PEPPERS, AVOCADO, AND MANGOES

SERVES 6

1 red bell pepper
1 yellow bell pepper
1 green bell pepper
12 cherry tomatoes
1 tablespoon olive oil
1 1/2 pounds fresh sea scallops
1/4 cup fresh lime juice
1/4 cup gold tequila
1/3 cup chopped fresh cilantro
1/3 cup chopped fresh basil
3 tablespoons chilled unsalted butter, cut into pieces
1 cup diced peeled pitted avocado
1 cup diced peeled pitted mango
fresh cilantro sprigs

METHOD

Char bell peppers over gas flame or in broiler until blackened on all sides. Enclose in paper bag; let stand 10 minutes. Peel and seed bell peppers. Cut all bell peppers into matchstick-size strips. Set aside.

Arrange tomatoes on baking sheet. Broil until tomatoes begin to brown and blister, about 5 minutes.

Heat oil in heavy large skillet over high heat. Add scallops and cook 2 minutes. Remove from heat. Turn scallops over. Add lime juice to skillet, then tequila. Simmer until scallops are cooked through and liquid is reduced to half, about 2 minutes. Using slotted spoon, transfer scallops to plate. Stir roasted peppers, tomatoes, cilantro, and basil into cooking liquid. Add butter 1 piece at a time, whisking just until melted. Return scallops to skillet. Season to taste with salt and pepper.

Spoon the scallop mixture onto the plates. Sprinkle with diced avocado and mango. Garnish with cilantro sprigs.

GRILLED OYSTERS WITH MANGO
PICO DE GALLO

SERVES 6

1 ripe mango, peeled, pitted, and cut into very small dice
1/2 red onion, peeled and cut into very small dice
1 small jalapeno, cut into very small dice
1 lime, juiced
2 tablespoons extra-virgin olive oil
2 teaspoons honey
2 tablespoons chopped cilantro leaves
salt and freshly ground pepper
1/2 cup prepared horseradish, drained
1 1/2 tablespoons chili powder
salt
20 oysters, scrubbed well

METHOD

To make Mango Pico de Gallo, mix together the mango, onion, jalapeno, lime juice, oil, honey, and cilantro in a medium bowl. Season it with salt and pepper to taste. Let it sit at room temperature for 30 minutes before using.

Mix together the horseradish and chili powder in a small bowl. Season it with salt.

Heat grill to high. Dip oysters in water, as this will help them steam open on the grill. Place oysters on the grill, close the cover, and grill until all have opened, about 3 to 4 minutes. Discard any that do not open. Place a tablespoon of the Mango Pico de Gallo on top of each oyster and top that with a scant teaspoon of the red horseradish.

BBQ BURGER WITH MANGO KETCHUP

<u>SERVES 4</u>

Burgers

1 pound finely ground meat
1 cup barbeque sauce
salt and pepper
4 hamburger buns

Mango Ketchup

2 tablespoons olive oil
1 small onion, coarsely chopped
2 cloves garlic, coarsely chopped
1 mango, peeled and coarsely chopped
1/4 teaspoon ground cinnamon
1/4 teaspoon allspice
pinch of ground cloves
1 habanero pepper, coarsely chopped
1/2 cup red wine vinegar
1 teaspoon honey
salt and freshly ground pepper

<u>METHOD</u>

Divide the meat into fourths and shape into burgers. Brush on both sides with the barbeque sauce and season with salt and pepper to taste. Grill for 3 to 4 minutes on each side.

Heat oil in a medium saucepan over medium-high heat. Add onions and garlic and cook until soft. Add mango and cook for 5 minutes, or until soft. Add cinnamon, allspice, cloves, and habanero and cook an additional 2 minutes. Place the mango mixture in a food processor and add the vinegar and honey. Process until smooth and consistent.

Season it with salt and pepper. Serve cold or at room temperature with BBQ burgers.

CONDIMENTS

Mango and Red Pepper Chutney

Mango Raita

Mango Papaya Salsa

Mango and Red Pepper Barbeque Sauce

Mango and Dried Fruit Chutney

Green Mango Pickle

Mango Vinaigrette

MANGO AND RED PEPPER CHUTNEY

This chutney can be served with grilled meats, curries, and sandwiches. Store it in an airtight container up to 2 months in a refrigerator.

MAKES ABOUT 4 CUPS

3 firm-ripe mangoes (3 lb total), peeled, pitted, and cut into 1/2-inch cubes

1/3 cup distilled white vinegar

1/3 cup packed dark brown sugar

1/3 cup golden raisins

1 3/4 teaspoons salt

1 (1-inch) piece fresh ginger, peeled and chopped

1 tablespoon chopped fresh jalapeno including seeds (from 1 chile)

3 garlic cloves, chopped

3/4 teaspoon ground cumin

3/4 teaspoon ground coriander

1/2 teaspoon turmeric

2 tablespoons vegetable oil

1 medium onion, chopped

1 red bell pepper, cut into 1/4-inch dice

1 (3-inch) cinnamon stick

METHOD

Toss together mangoes, vinegar, brown sugar, raisins, and a teaspoon salt.

Mince together ginger, jalapeno, and garlic to a paste with remaining 3/4 teaspoon salt using a large heavy knife, then stir in cumin, coriander, and turmeric.

Heat oil in a heavy pot over moderately high heat. Sauté onion and bell pepper, stirring occasionally, until golden, 8 to 10 minutes. Add garlic paste and cinnamon stick, and then reduce heat to moderate and cook, stirring, 1 minute.

Stir in mango mixture and simmer, covered, stirring occasionally, until mangoes are tender, about 30 minutes. Discard cinnamon stick and cool chutney, uncovered, about 45 minutes.

MANGO RAITA

Raita, an Indian yogurt dish used as a condiment, is often made with cucumber or tomatoes. This version has mango. Serve it with grilled pork or fish.

MAKES ABOUT 2 CUPS

1/4 English cucumber, diced (about 1 cup)
1 mango, peeled, diced (about 1 cup)
1/4 cup plain yogurt
2 tablespoons thinly sliced fresh mint leaves
2 teaspoons honey

METHOD

Toss all ingredients in medium bowl to combine. Raita can be prepared 1 day ahead. Cover and refrigerate.

MANGO PAPAYA SALSA

This salsa can be made up to 6 hours in advance and stored in the refrigerator.

MAKES ABOUT 3 CUPS

2 cups chopped pitted peeled mango
1 cup diced firm papaya
1 cup chopped red bell pepper
2/3 cup chopped green onions
1/4 cup chopped fresh cilantro
2 tablespoons fresh lime juice
4 teaspoons olive oil

METHOD

Mix all ingredients in small bowl. Season it with salt and pepper.

MANGO AND RED PEPPER BARBEQUE SAUCE

This sauce is a perfect accompaniment with grilled seafood or chicken.

MAKES ABOUT 1 1/2 CUPS

2 tablespoons olive oil
1 medium onion, chopped
1 medium red bell pepper, chopped
1 teaspoon salt
1/3 cup red-wine vinegar
3 tablespoons molasses
2 tablespoons Worcestershire sauce
1/4 teaspoon ground allspice
1 medium mango (about 1 pound), cut into chunks
2 to 3 fresh jalapeno chilies, or to taste, seeded (wear rubber gloves)

METHOD

In a skillet, heat oil over moderate heat until hot, but not smoking, and cook onion and bell pepper with salt until softened and edges begin to brown. Stir in vinegar, molasses, Worcestershire sauce, and allspice and bring to a boil. Simmer mixture 1 minute to blend flavors and cool slightly.

Spoon the mixture into a blender. Add mango and jalapenos and blend until smooth.

MANGO AND DRIED FRUIT CHUTNEY

The mangoes must be completely unripe in order to achieve the firm, chunky texture desired for this chutney.

MAKES ABOUT 4 CUPS

3 unripe mangoes (about 3 pounds total)
1 1/4 cup chopped dried fruits, mixed (raisins, apricots, prunes, or any choice)
1/2 cup distilled vinegar
1/3 cup sugar plus additional to taste if mango is very sour
1 1/2 teaspoons salt, or to taste
1-inch piece fresh gingerroot, peeled
2 fresh Thai (bird) chilies or 1 fresh jalapeno chili
5 garlic cloves
1 teaspoon ground cumin
1 teaspoon ground coriander seeds
1/2 teaspoon ground turmeric
3-inch piece cinnamon stick
2 star anise
2 tablespoons corn oil

METHOD

Peel mangoes and cut into 1/2-inch cubes. In a small bowl, toss mangoes with dried fruits, vinegar, sugar, and salt.

Cut gingerroot into 4 pieces. For milder chutney, wearing rubber gloves, remove seeds from Thai chilies or jalapeno. To a food processor with motor running, add gingerroot, chilies, cloves, cumin, coriander, and turmeric, one at a time through feed tube, and purée to a paste.

Heat a 4-quart, heavy kettle over moderately low heat until hot. Cook seasoning paste, cinnamon stick, and star anise in oil, stirring frequently for 10 minutes, or until very fragrant.

Stir in mango mixture and simmer, covered, over low heat, stirring occasionally, until mangoes are tender, about 20 minutes. Discard cinnamon stick and star anise and cool chutney completely. Chutney keeps, covered and chilled, about 1 month.

GREEN MANGO PICKLE

This is a very common traditional Indian condiment. Fenugreek seeds are available in spice markets or Indian stores.

MAKES ABOUT 6 CUPS

4 raw green mangoes
3 tablespoons fenugreek seeds
4 tablespoons fennel seeds
2 tablespoons red chili powder
2 tablespoons turmeric powder
3 tablespoons mustard seeds
2 cups mustard oil
salt as per taste

METHOD

Cut raw mangoes into half, remove seed, and then cut 3/4-inch-sized pieces.

Apply turmeric powder and salt, rub nicely, and then keep it for half an hour. Drain out excess moisture.

Grind fenugreek seeds, fennel seeds, and mustard seeds to a coarse powder.

Heat mustard oil until smoking point, remove, and let it cool.

Mix fenugreek seeds, fennel, and mustard powder with red chili powder. Add half of the mustard oil to this mixture and rub this spice and oil mixture to the mango pieces. Mix thoroughly.

Put this into an earthenware jar and pour the remaining mustard oil. Cover the jar with a muslin cloth and keep it in the sun for 5-6 days.

Make sure you stir the contents of the jar for the first two weeks at least once a day. This is to ensure that the mango pieces are always in contact with the oil.

MANGO VINAIGRETTE

This is very refreshing for a summer salad. Serve it with mixed arugula or Bibb lettuce with grilled shrimp, scallops, or chicken breast.

MAKES ABOUT 3 CUPS

1 medium-ripe mango, peeled and cut
2 tablespoons minced ginger
2 tablespoons lime juice
1/4 cup rice vinegar
1 small red pepper, diced
1 small Thai red chili, chopped
1/4 cup cilantro
1/4 cup canola oil
salt and pepper to taste

METHOD

Combine mango, ginger, lime juice, and vinegar and process until smooth. Combine this mixture with other ingredients except oil. Gradually whisk in oil and create an emulsion. This vinaigrette will keep, covered in the refrigerator for 2-3 days.

DESSERTS

Mango and Blueberry Pavlovas

Mango Cheesecake

Mango Coconut Ice Cream

Mango Crème Brulee

Mango Upside-Down Cake

Mango Strudel with Vanilla Lime Sauce

Mangoes with Sticky Rice

Shrikhand

Mango Sorbet

Mango Tart Tatin

Mango Cobbler

Mango Pie

MANGO AND BLUEBERRY PAVLOVAS

If apple pie is America's classic dessert, then this is Australia's. The meringues are a little tricky to cook since they need a short period of high heat to set and crisp the exterior, and then a longer period at lower heat, so the interior is set but still chewy. It's best not to make meringues on humid days when it is practically impossible to get anything other than a soggy result.

SERVES 6

4 large egg whites, at room temperature
1 cup superfine sugar, plus more for sprinkling
1 tablespoon fresh lemon juice
2 teaspoons cornstarch
1 teaspoon pure vanilla extract
1 large ripe mango, peeled, fruit cut off the pit, thinly sliced
1 cup blueberries
1 cup heavy cream
confectioners' sugar, for dusting

METHOD

Preheat the oven to 325 degrees F. Line a large baking sheet with parchment paper or foil. In a large bowl, beat the egg whites at medium speed until soft peaks form. Beat in the superfine sugar, 1 tablespoon at a time, and continue beating until the meringue is thick, glossy, and stiff.

Quickly beat in 2 teaspoons of the lemon juice, the cornstarch, and the vanilla. Spoon the meringue into 6 evenly spaced mounds on the parchment-lined sheet. Using the tip of the spoon, make a well in each meringue.

Bake the meringues for 5 minutes, or until slightly dry and set. Reduce the temperature to 225 degrees F. Bake for 1 hour. Turn off the oven and leave the meringues in the oven for 1 hour with the oven door closed. The meringues should be perfectly white and crisp on the outside but chewy inside.

Toss the mango slices and blueberries with the remaining 1 teaspoon of lemon juice and sprinkle with superfine sugar if desired. Set the meringues on dessert plates. Whip the heavy cream and spoon onto the meringues. Top with the mango slices and blueberries, sift confectioners' sugar over the tops and serve at once.

MANGO CHEESECAKE

Pureed fresh mango gives this cheesecake a light and soft texture and subtle tropical fruit flavor.

SERVES 12

Crust

1 1/2 cups graham cracker crumbs
1/2 cup sugar
6 tablespoons (3/4 stick) unsalted butter, melted

Filling

3 large very ripe mangoes (each about 13 ounces), peeled, pitted, coarsely chopped
3 8-ounce packages cream cheese, room temperature
1 1/4 cups sugar
2 teaspoons vanilla extract
4 large eggs
sliced peeled pitted mangoes

METHOD

Preheat oven to 325 degrees F. Lightly butter 9-inch-diameter spring form pan with 2 3/4-inch-high sides. Stir cracker crumbs and sugar in medium bowl to blend. Add melted butter and stir until evenly moistened. Press crumb mixture firmly onto bottom (not sides) of prepared pan. Bake until crust is set, about 12 minutes. Cool completely. Maintain oven temperature.

Puree mangoes in processor until smooth. Set aside 2 cups mango purée (reserve any remaining purée for another use). Beat cream cheese, sugar, and vanilla in large bowl until smooth. Add eggs, 1 at a time, beating

64

well after each addition. Add 2 cups mango purée and beat until well blended. Pour filling over crust in pan.

Bake cake until set and puffed and golden around edges (center may move very slightly when pan is gently shaken), about 1 hour 25 minutes. Cool cake 1 hour. Refrigerate uncovered overnight.

Run small knife between cake and sides of pan to loosen. Remove pan sides. Transfer cake to platter. Cut into wedges and serve with sliced mangoes.

MANGO COCONUT ICE CREAM

In Thailand, mangoes often appear on the table for dessert, served both on their own and incorporated into sweetened sticky rice. If you can't get your hands on really good mangoes, you'll find that canned mango purée delivers the best flavor for this ice cream. However, many canned brands taste like peaches, so we recommend Ratna brand, which uses Alphonso mangoes, an Indian cultivar renowned for its bright orange flesh and very intense flavor. Ka-Me brand is a runner-up— the recipe will work fine, but the color and flavor will not be as intense.

MAKES ABOUT 1 1/2 QUARTS

1 1/4 cups canned mango purée
3/4 cup well-stirred canned unsweetened coconut milk
1/2 cup heavy cream
2 tablespoons light corn syrup
1 tablespoon fresh lemon juice
1/4 teaspoon vanilla
1 cup whole milk
2 large egg yolks
1/2 cup sugar
special equipment: an instant-read thermometer; an ice cream maker

METHOD

Stir together mango purée, coconut milk, cream, corn syrup, lemon juice, and vanilla in a bowl until combined well.

Bring milk just to a boil in a 2- to 3-quart heavy saucepan. Whisk together yolks, sugar, and a large pinch of salt in a bowl, then add hot milk in a stream, whisking. Pour custard into saucepan and cook over moderately low heat, stirring with a wooden spoon, until it registers 170°F to 175°F on thermometer, 2 to 3 minutes. Remove from heat, and then stir in mango mixture until combined well.

Pour custard through a fine-mesh sieve into a large bowl (to remove any strings from mango), discarding solids, and cool to room temperature, stirring occasionally. Chill the custard, covered, until very cold, about 4 hours.

Freeze custard in ice cream maker. Transfer ice cream to an airtight container and put in freezer to harden, at least 12 hours.

MANGO CRÈME BRULEE

SERVES 6

5 large egg yolks
1/3 cup granulated sugar
1/8 teaspoon salt
1 vanilla bean, halved lengthwise
2 cups heavy cream
1 1/2 cups diced (1/4-inch) firm-ripe mango (from 1 1/2 lb)
3 tablespoons sugar
special equipment: 6 (4-oz) flameproof ramekins

METHOD

Preheat oven to 325 degrees F.

Whisk together yolks, granulated sugar, and salt in a bowl until combined well. Using tip of a knife, scrape seeds from vanilla bean into cream in a 2-quart saucepan, then add pod. Heat over moderate heat until hot but not boiling. Discard pod and add cream to egg mixture in a slow stream, whisking until combined.

Spoon 1/4 cup mango into each ramekin. Pour custard through a fine-mesh sieve into a bowl, then ladle over mango. Arrange ramekins in a roasting pan and bake in a hot water bath in middle of oven until custards are just set, 35 to 40 minutes. Transfer custards with tongs to a rack to cool, then chill, uncovered, at least 4 hours. Preheat broiler.

Sprinkle sugar evenly over custards and broil in a shallow baking pan 5 to 7 inches from heat until sugar is caramelized, 2 to 3 minutes.

MANGO UPSIDE-DOWN CAKE

SERVES 6

For Topping

2 (1-lb) firm-ripe mangoes, peeled
1/2 stick (1/4 cup) unsalted butter
1/2 cup packed light brown sugar

For Cake Batter

1 1/2 cups all-purpose flour
1 teaspoon baking powder
1/4 teaspoon salt
1 stick (1/2 cup) unsalted butter, softened
1 cup granulated sugar
3 large eggs, 2 of them separated
1 teaspoon vanilla
1/2 cup mango purée

METHOD

Standing each mango upright, remove flesh from pit by cutting a thick lengthwise slice from each broad side. Put slices on a work surface and cut lengthwise into 3/8-inch-thick slices.

Melt butter in a small heavy saucepan over moderate heat, and then stir in brown sugar. Simmer, stirring, until butter is incorporated, 1 to 2 minutes. Spread mixture in bottom of a buttered 9- by 2-inch round baking pan and arrange mango on top, overlapping slices.

Preheat oven to 350 degrees F.

Whisk together flour, baking powder, and salt. Beat together butter and sugar in a large bowl with an electric mixer at high speed until light and fluffy, about 6 minutes. Add whole egg and yolks, 1 at a time, beating well after each addition. Beat in vanilla. Add half of flour mixture and mix at low speed until just combined. Mix in mango purée, add remaining flour mixture, mixing until just combined.

Beat egg whites in another bowl with cleaned beaters until they just hold stiff peaks, then fold into batter gently but thoroughly.

Gently spoon the batter over mango topping and spread it evenly. Bake in middle of oven until golden brown and a tester comes out clean, 55 to 60 minutes. Cool cake in pan on a rack 10 minutes. Run a thin knife around inside edge of pan, then invert a plate over pan and invert cake onto plate. Cool completely on plate on rack.

Serve the cake at room temperature.

MANGO STRUDEL WITH VANILLA LIME SAUCE

SERVES 8

For the Strudel

3 mangoes (1 pound each) cut into 1-inch chunks (3 cups)

2 to 3 tablespoons sugar, depending upon sweetness of the fruit

6 tablespoons dry breadcrumbs

1/2 cup finely chopped pecans

6 sheets of frozen, thawed phyllo leaves (16 x 2 inches each)

6 tablespoons melted butter for phyllo dough

6 tablespoons melted unsalted butter

For the Sauce

2 cups melted vanilla ice cream

6 tablespoons fresh lime juice

METHOD

Preheat the oven to 400 degrees F. In a mixing bowl, combine the mangoes, sugar, lime zest, 2 tablespoons of breadcrumbs, and pecans.

Spread the phyllo leaves on a damp cloth towel covering the top with another damp towel so the leaves do not dry out as you are working.

Place one phyllo leaf on a clean dry cloth towel and brush it with melted butter using a pastry brush. Sprinkle the dough with 2 teaspoons dry breadcrumbs. Place a second leaf of phyllo on top, brush with melted butter, and sprinkle with breadcrumbs. Repeat this procedure with all of the phyllo leaves.

Place the mango filling in a 3-inch strip along the longer edge of the dough, to within 1 1/2 inches of the sides. Fold the sides over the filling and roll the dough into a jellyroll shape using the cloth to help you.

Transfer the strudel onto a non-stick baking sheet, seam side down. Brush the top with melted butter and bake for about 25 minutes or until golden brown. Remove from the oven and cool for 30 minutes before serving.

Right before serving the strudel, blend the ice cream with the lime juice. Spoon 2 to 3 tablespoons of sauce on a plate and center a slice of strudel in the sauce. Dust some confectioners' sugar over the strudel slice and serve immediately to enjoy the contrast between the warm strudel dough and the cool sauce.

MANGOES WITH STICKY RICE

SERVES 8

2 cups glutinous rice
2 1/4 cups water
1 1/4 cups coconut cream
2/3 cup sugar
1/2 teaspoon salt
banana leaves, rinsed and patted dry (optional)
2 mangoes, peeled, pitted and thickly sliced, chilled
toasted, unsweetened, shredded dried coconut or
chopped dry-roasted peanuts for garnish

METHOD

Rinse the rice thoroughly with water until the rinse water
runs clear. Drain. Place the rice in a saucepan and add
the 2 1/4 cups water. Let soak for at least 2 hours or as
long as overnight.

Bring the rice to a boil over high heat. Stir to loosen the
grains from the bottom of the pan. Continue to boil until
all the water on the surface is absorbed, 3-5 minutes.
Cover, reduce the heat to low, and simmer for 20
minutes. Remove from the heat and let the rice stand,
covered, for at least 10 minutes or up to 40 minutes
before stirring. The rice should be plumped, tender, and
sticky. Transfer to a large bowl and set aside.

In a saucepan, combine the coconut cream, sugar, and
salt and bring to a boil over high heat. Boil, stirring
constantly, until reduced to a thick cream, about 5
minutes. Pour the coconut cream over the rice and gently
blend together.

Line each individual dessert plate with a banana leaf, if desired. Mound about 3/4 cup of the sticky rice on each leaf. Arrange mango slices around the mounds. Sprinkle with toasted coconut or peanuts and serve.

SHRIKHAND

Here's a classic Indian dessert, made with drained yogurt, cardamom, and saffron. The saffron is toasted until brittle so that you can grind it easily. If you grind your own cardamom seeds, use only half a teaspoon instead of the quantity in our recipe.

SERVES 4

small pinch saffron
1 quart plain whole-milk yogurt
3/4 teaspoon ground cardamom
2 tablespoons water
1/3 cup powdered sugar, or more to taste
1/4 cup shredded unsweetened coconut
1 mango, peeled, pitted, cut into thin slices

METHOD

In a small pan, toast the saffron over low heat, stirring, until brittle, about 2 minutes. Remove and pulverize in a mortar with a pestle or on a cutting board with the side of a large knife blade.

Put the yogurt in a large bowl. Put the saffron back into the pan and add the cardamom and water. Bring just to a simmer, stirring. Whisk the saffron mixture into the yogurt.

Put the yogurt mixture in a strainer lined with cheesecloth, a coffee filter, or a paper towel and set it over a bowl. Let drain in the refrigerator for 1 hour. Transfer the yogurt to a bowl. Add the 1/3 cup sugar, or more, to taste. With an electric mixer, beat the yogurt until slightly thickened, 2 to 3 minutes. Pour into bowls and refrigerate until well chilled, or put in the freezer until very cold, but not frozen, about 30 minutes.

Meanwhile, in a small frying pan, toast the coconut over low heat, stirring, until golden, about 2 minutes.

Serve the shrikhand topped with the mango and coconut.

MANGO SORBET

SERVES 6

1 cup sugar
3/4 cup water
2 ripe mangoes, about 1/2 lb each
juice of 1 lime

METHOD

Combine the sugar and water in a small saucepan and place over low heat. Stir until the sugar dissolves completely and the syrup is clear. Remove from the heat and allow cooling to room temperature.

Peel the mangoes and cut as much of the fruit as you can away from the large pits. If the mangoes are very ripe and juicy, and you feel adventurous, squeeze the pulp and juice off the pits with your hands. It's messy work, so do it over a large bowl.

Combine the cooled syrup, mango pulp, and lime juice in a blender or food processor. Blend until completely smooth, about 30 seconds. Cover and refrigerate until cold, or overnight.

Stir the chilled mixture, and then freeze in your ice cream machine, according to the manufacturer's instructions. When finished, the sorbet will be soft, but ready to eat. For firmer sorbet, transfer to a freezer-safe container and freeze at least 2 hours.

MANGO TART TATIN

2 cups all-purpose flour
5 ounces unsalted butter
1 egg yolk
3 tablespoons powdered sugar
1/2 teaspoon salt
4 to 6 tablespoons cold water
1 cup sugar
1/2 cup water
3 large mangoes, not too ripe
2 tablespoons melted butter

METHOD

Make pastry dough by placing flour, butter, egg yolk, powdered sugar, and salt in food processor and pulsing until texture resembles a course meal. Add water, tablespoon by tablespoon. Assemble dough into small ball, wrap in plastic film, and flatten to 1-inch circle. Chill for 30 minutes.

Roll out dough and cut into 4 1/4-inch rounds and let chill for another 30 minutes.

Preheat oven to 400 degrees F.

Make caramel in non-reactive pan with sugar and water. Heat 6 (5-inch) cast-iron pans, or 6 (8-ounce) ramekins in the oven.

When sugar and water are a warm amber color, place pan in bowl of cold water to stop cooking. Pour caramel into hot pans and fill with mango slices.

Brush mango slices with melted butter. Prick pastry rounds with fork and place on top of mangoes. Bake it in a 400-degree oven for 25 minutes, or until pastry is browned.

MANGO COBBLER

SERVES 6

2/3 cup sugar

1 tablespoon cornstarch

1 cup water

3 cups sliced mangoes

1 cup flour

1 teaspoon lemon juice

1 tablespoon granulated sugar mixed with 1 teaspoon cinnamon

1 1/2 teaspoon baking powder

1/2 teaspoon salt

3 tablespoons shortening

1/2 cup milk

1 1/2 teaspoon margarine

METHOD

Mix sugar and cornstarch in saucepan, and gradually stir in water and fruit and lemon juice. Heat, stirring well. Pour into 1 1/2 qt. baking dish; dot with margarine and sprinkle sugar cinnamon mixture over the top.

Stir together flour, sugar, baking powder, and salt. Cut in shortening until mixture looks like meal. Now stir in milk. Mix well.

Drop by spoonfuls on to hot fruit. Bake 20 to 30 minutes. Serve warm or cold.

MANGO PIE

This is a quick and easy mango pie recipe.

SERVES 6

2 1/2 cups peeled and sliced ripe mango
2 tablespoons quick-cooking tapioca
3/4 cup granulated sugar
1/4 teaspoon salt
1 tablespoon melted butter
2 pie shells, pre-baked

METHOD

Combine mango slices, tapioca, sugar, salt, and melted butter. Toss to combine; let stand for 15 to 20 minutes. Roll out half of the pastry very thin; line a 9-inch pie pan, trim the edge. Roll out the remaining pastry very thin. Fill the shell with fruit mixture.

Moisten edge of crust. Place the top crust on filling; make several slits in top to vent steam. Trim top crust leaving it just a little larger than the pan. Press top crust and moistened bottom crust edge together; fold excess top under the bottom edge. Flute all around rim. Bake mango pie at 425 degrees F for about 50 to 60 minutes, or until top is well browned.

Cut it into pieces and serve it hot or cold.

DRINKS

Mango Lassi

Mango-Boysenberry Mimosa

Mango Daiquiri

Mango Martini

Mango Mint Mojito

MANGO LASSI

In Indian restaurants, lassi is served with the meal, but we frequently find this exotic "smoothie" too filling to accompany a main course and prefer it in place of dessert. Look for the smaller, yellow-skinned mangoes, which have a more pronounced flavor than the larger, red and green ones.

SERVES 4

2 1/2 cups chopped peeled mango (from about 2 1/2 lb very ripe mangoes)
1/4 cup sugar
1 quart well-shaken buttermilk
garnish: lime wedges

METHOD

Purée mango with sugar in a blender until smooth. Add buttermilk and blend well. Force through a very fine sieve into a large glass measure. Serve lassi over ice in tall glasses.

MANGO-BOYSENBERRY MIMOSA

Brunch drinks get updated with this take on the traditional duo of orange juice and champagne. Note that freshly squeezed orange juice is not the best choice here, as its intense taste can overwhelm the other juices. Topping the drink with a boysenberry "floater" creates a vibrant color contrast.

SERVES 10

2 cups frozen unsweetened boysenberry, thawed

2 tablespoons sugar

3 cups chilled orange juice (do not use freshly squeezed)

1 1/2 cups frozen orange-peach-mango juice concentrate

1 750-ml bottle of chilled dry champagne

10 small orange slices

METHOD

Place 10 berries in freezer; reserve for garnish. Purée remaining berries in processor. Strain through a sieve over a bowl, pressing on the solids. Mix in sugar. (Purée can be made 1 day ahead.) Cover and refrigerate.

Whisk orange juice and concentrate in pitcher to blend. Mix in champagne. Divide mimosa among 10 champagne glasses. Drizzle 1 1/2 teaspoons berry purée over each.

Garnish with orange slices and reserved berries.

MANGO DAIQUIRI

This is famous in Cuba, a country well known for its high quality rum and flavorful mangoes.

SERVES 4

3/4 cup mangoes, peeled and sliced
3 tablespoons freshly squeezed lime juice
3 tablespoons sugar
1/2 cup white or dark rum
4 cups ice

METHOD

Combine all ingredients in blender until smooth and serve chilled.

Happy drinking.

MANGO MARTINI

SERVES 2

ice cubes
1 cup Mango Vodka
2 twists of lime zest

Put the ice cubes in a shaker glass. Put the vodka over the
ice cubes and shake well. Strain into 2 well-chilled
martini glasses. Garnish with a lime twist.

MANGO VODKA

Peel 3 ripe mangoes, cut the flesh from the pit, and cut
into large dice. Put the mangoes in a clean quart Mason
jar. Add 2 cups vodka and seal the jar. Let it sit in a cool
dark place for 2 to 3 days before using. Store the leftover
vodka up to 5 days.

MANGO MINT MOJITO

Use ripe mangoes or sweetened mango purée to get the sweet aroma of the tropics.

SERVES 4

1 cup ice
6 ounces light rum
1 cup chopped mangoes or mango purée
12 mint sprigs
6 tablespoons fresh lime juice
4 tablespoons sugar
club soda
4 slices lime

METHOD

Place ice in a beverage shaker, then add the rum, mango purée, and sugar. Shake well and serve in a highball glass, topped with a splash of club soda.

Garnish each with a slice of lime.

A part of Author's Royalties will be generously donated to

MOTHER TERESA'S – "MISSIONARIES OF CHARITY, INDIA"

Lightning Source UK Ltd.
Milton Keynes UK
UKOW040610060713

213343UK00012B/446/A

9 780741 424839